IMAGES
of England

SHIPWRECKS
OF KENT

The lifeboat *Bradford* (II) that saved the crew of the *Indian Chief*, wrecked on the Long Sand in 1881, drawn up on the East Pier slipway at Ramsgate. This was a magnificent rescue performed in a boat that offered very little protection from the elements.

IMAGES
of England

SHIPWRECKS
OF KENT

Anthony Lane

I dedicate this book to my wife, Jean,
for her help and encouragement.
Also to our cat, Casey, in spite of whose assistance
the work was completed on time.

TEMPUS

First published 1999
Reprinted 2000, 2006

Tempus Publishing Limited
The Mill, Brimscombe Port,
Stroud, Gloucestershire, GL5 2QG
www.tempus-publishing.com

British Library Cataloguing in Publication Data.
A catalogue record for this book is available from the British Library.

ISBN 978 0 7524 1720 2

Typesetting and origination by Tempus Publishing Limited.
Printed in Great Britain.

Contents

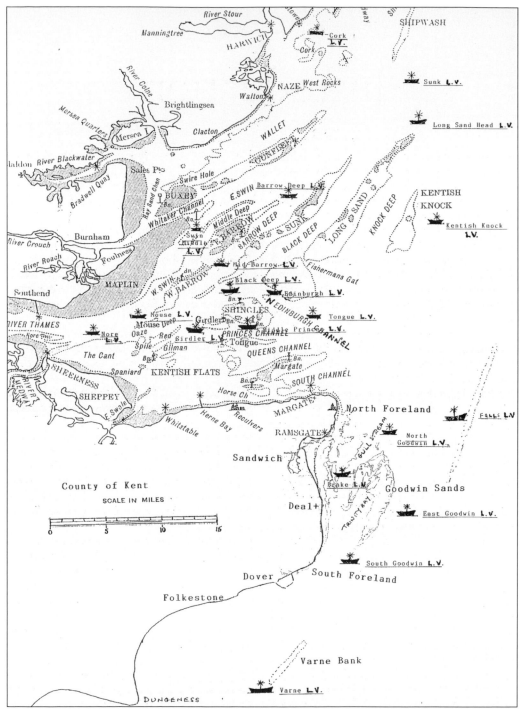

This chart of the Kent coast and Thames estuary indicates the approximate locations of the sandbanks. The different lightvessels that have at one time or another provided a warning of these hazards are also shown.

Introduction

As an introductory statement it has to be admitted that any work that attempts to describe shipping casualties on the coast of Kent can only hope to scratch the surface of the subject. So many wrecks have occurred, particularly during the time of sailing vessels, that no complete list can ever be compiled. Many wooden ships disappeared without trace and others might sometimes receive a brief notice in a missing vessel's report once Lloyds started to record shipping losses.

Any pictorial record is further limited to those wrecks that were captured by artists or, later, by photographers. To some extent the painting of shipwrecks became popular during the nineteenth century and by the use of engravings these could be transferred to the printed page. Journals such as *The Illustrated London News* and *The Graphic* regularly published accounts of lost ships together with any heroic action of those that saved the crews. Even so the event had usually to have disastrous proportions before it was given much space. The most notorious shipwrecks therefore make up the greater part of this book.

Having stated some of the limitations as to why relatively few early shipwrecks were recorded for posterity, it is important to state that the photographic camera did make a considerable difference to the number of these events that were recorded. Hence, from around 1870 onwards pictures of wrecked vessels become more abundant.

In spite of these restrictions, however, there have been so many wrecks around the south-east coast that a wide range of pictures is available and a number of the more famous casualties have been the subject of a whole series of photographs.

Certain areas of Kent have gained notoriety for the number of vessels that have perished in that region. At the top of any list come the Goodwin Sands, famous since medieval times as the 'Great Ship Swallower' and referred to even by Shakespeare. Although it is claimed that more ships have been wrecked there than any equivalent area of the British Isles, the sandbanks of the Thames estuary, extending eastwards like the palm of a hand, have also taken a considerable toll. Although not a scenic estuary, finding the deep-water channels between them has always made the approach to the port of London an interesting project for the navigator.

Many of the earlier casualties were caused either by stress of weather or poor navigation, or a combination of the two. A severe north-easterly gale could cause havoc to sailing vessels particularly if they had previously been sheltering in Margate Roads or the Downs from a strong westerly wind. Later, the advent of steam power brought two advantages: firstly, the availability of tugs that could assist vessels and prevent them from drifting into danger; secondly, steam-powered iron ships could hold their course much better in high winds and strong tides. They equally stood a better chance of surviving a stranding due to the increased strength of their hull. Once steel ships became commonplace one finds numerous views of vessels high and dry which subsequently were salved when the tide returned.

As the coast of Kent is long and so many wrecks have occurred, this introduction and the pictures included in this volume are divided into different sections, namely, *The North Kent Coast*, comprising the River Thames and coastline from Woolwich to the eastern extremity of the county at Margate, *The Goodwin Sands*, which is self-explanatory, and *The East Kent Coast*, covering the stretch of mainland coast from Margate to Dungeness. This part includes the English Channel casualties. A final part of this pictorial history, entitled *Kent Lifeboats to the Rescue*, is devoted to the development of life saving on the coast and the large part played by the Royal National Lifeboat Institution. This part is sub-divided into the different towns from which lifeboats operate.

Superimposed on all aspects of this work is a third factor, totally separate from weather and inaccurate navigation. This is the impact of enemy action during two world wars. Numerous mines were laid by the Germans in the shipping lanes around Kent in both wars and allied losses were high among merchant ships and minesweepers alike. Photography was not usually permitted during periods of hostilities, but it is surprising how many pictures have become available of ships sinking after striking mines. A further factor that contributed to losses was the use of the Downs as a contraband control area where all neutral ships were brought in for examination. The resulting congestion close to the Goodwins led to more than a few ships being lost due to collision or inadvertently running aground on the Sands. Losses also occurred in the Straits of Dover and eastern English Channel during the Second World War from German air attacks on convoys. Many colliers were sunk in this way between Deal and Dungeness.

Having set the scene generally, the various areas can now be examined in more detail and attention given to wrecks that have attracted more than the average public interest.

The North Kent Coast.

Being such a busy and important waterway, the River Thames has had its fair share of shipwrecks over the years. However, the most costly in human life and most harrowing was the loss of the crowded paddle steamer *Princess Alice* off Margaret Ness on 3 September 1878. Having come into collision with the steamer *Bywell Castle*, the pleasure vessel sank very quickly, taking about 640 of her passengers down with her. Recovery of the bodies proved a gruesome task as the ship had sunk close to the northern sewage outfall at Beckton. The loss of the *Princess Alice* had a direct impact on the decision to take the London waste out to sea for dumping.

Fortunately there have been no other cases to compare with the foregoing in the London River but serious losses of life have occurred more frequently in the Thames estuary. On 28 February 1849 the American barque *Floridian*, carrying German emigrants to the United States, struck the Long Sand off Harwich in a gale with hail and snow squalls. She soon broke up. Only four of the 197 passengers and crew aboard were saved. Only just over a year later, on 30 March 1850, the Dublin packet steamer *Royal Adelaide*, 450 tons, drove on to the Tongue Sand off Margate 'in terrific seas,' and was lost with her crew of twenty-four and twelve passengers (some sources give 428 persons lost).

It is important to recall one further disaster, that of the North German Lloyd liner *Deutschland* which struck the Kentish Knock, the most easterly of the Thames sandbanks, during snowstorms on 6 December 1875. Although the Kentish Knock lightship fired rockets and an organised lifesaving service was in existence, it took time for the remote position of the wreck to be communicated to the land. When the tug *Liverpool* arrived at the wreck the next day, fifty-seven of those aboard the *Deutschland* had already frozen to death in the rigging. The remaining 173 were saved.

Two major disasters took place in the River Medway during the First World War, which must receive a mention. A huge explosion destroyed the battleship *Bulwark* while she was at anchor in November 1914, near the present position of Bee Ness jetty, with a resultant loss of 729 men. In terms of cost in human life, this may have been the most tragic single shipwreck in Kent. Only six months later a similar blast totally destroyed the new minelayer *Princess Irene* while she was loading mines in Saltpan Reach, this time with over three hundred killed.

Two other interesting wrecks on the North Kent coast, more for their cargo, fortunately, than loss of life, were the East Indiamen, *Active* and *Hindostan*. Both were driven ashore in the same gale of January 1803, the former on the Margate foreshore and the latter on the Wedge Sand. Although the wrecks were fully explored at the time, more than usual interest has been shown over the years in prospecting for treasure from these vessels, as very little else of great value has been lost as a cause of shipwreck on the Thames banks since that date.

The loss of the barque *Hawksdale* on the Long Sand in 1899 is worth recalling, firstly because the crew were rescued in a heroic service by the Margate lifeboat and, secondly, because the hull of the ship has come back to haunt the seafarer of the present day. Due to the movement of the sandbanks, the North Edinburgh Channel, which was used for many years as the southern deep-water route to

London, has gradually moved north-eastwards. In recent years it has uncovered the 100-year-old wreck of the *Hawksdale*; the hulk eventually ending up in the middle of the channel where it has become a hazard to navigation and as a consequence has to be buoyed.

Although the offshore banks are highly dangerous, the chalk ledges and sand that occur from Reculver to Margate are relatively kind to stranded ships. This lee shore has offered some comfort to vessels driven southwards before the notorious north-easterly gales. On certain occasions, such as the storms of November 1877, the shoreline has been littered with craft, left high and dry when the tide receded, but, due to the soft nature of the rock, most have been successfully refloated over the years.

As a conclusion to this short history of the wrecks of north Kent one wartime wreck remains of great importance. On 20 August 1944 the American 'Liberty' ship *Richard Montgomery*, one of many carrying cargoes of munitions at that time, went aground on Sheerness Middle Sand about two miles from Garrison Point. Unlike those previously described, the ship remains relatively intact to this day together with about 4,000 tons of the bombs that comprised her original cargo, which provokes local press comment at regular intervals. She too is well buoyed, for she lies only about 1.5 cables from the Medway approach channel. In fact, the *Richard Montgomery* is the only wreck readily visible to the observer from any point on the Kent shore.

The Goodwin Sands

It is more difficult to choose the wrecks of greatest interest from this most notorious area for there are so many. In its recorded history, the greatest loss of life occurred during the great storm of 26-27 November 1703. The Naval vessels *Northumberland* (3rd rate), *Stirling Castle* (3rd rate), *Restoration* (3rd rate), and *Mary* (4th rate) were all lost on the Goodwin Sands along with Admiral Beaumont and about 1,200 of their crewmen. This must have been the 'storm of the millennium,' because the amount of damage inflicted on the south of England was incredible. Church steeples fell by the dozen, sheets of lead were rolled up on church roofs and nearby in Kent at the North Foreland lighthouse, the lightkeepers complained about blazing coals being blown from the brazier on to the ground below the tower. They must have had some fire going that night. This was a disaster incomparable with anything else that has occurred since on the Goodwins or anywhere else in Kent.

Not all shipwrecks were tragic; some had a humorous side, especially when regarded in hindsight. One stands out not for lifesaving or loss of life but for being part of a strange coincidence. On 9 April 1909 the Brocklebank steamer *Mahratta*, returning from the Far East, ran aground on the sandbank. Subsequently she broke up. Her cargo of tea was brought ashore to Deal and was to a large extent unofficially distributed about the cellars and attics of the town. Revenue men made random searches and some was discovered but there were also cases of blocked drains due to rapid disposal of the product when a knock came at the door. Thirty years later, on 6 October 1939, another *Mahratta* entered the Downs to pick up a pilot for the passage to London. Shortly afterwards her master wondered why the ship would not answer her helm. It was found that she too was aground, very close to where her predecessor had ended her days. This later *Mahratta* did not escape either and before long more tea began circulating in Deal. She had become one of the early casualties of the Second World War.

Tea was of relatively little benefit, however, compared to the cargo of the American 'Liberty' ship *Helena Modjeska*, which anchored in the Downs in September 1946 with a general cargo intended for northern Europe. Aboard the ship were very large quantities of tinned food including boned ham and turkey. Clothes were in abundance, while amassed on the deck was a veritable fleet of army lorries and various pieces of mobile road-making equipment such as bulldozers and cranes. At the time of departure her master made a grave error by trying to leave the Downs on a northerly heading, consequently running ashore on the Goodwins. Only a few days afterwards the ship broke in half. To the population of Deal, who had suffered shortages and rationing throughout the war years, this ship must have seemed a heaven-sent opportunity for salvage.

Boatmen came from as far away as Margate, Ramsgate and Dover, as well as the immediate locality, to assist with the recovery of the cargo. From contemporary accounts it would seem, perhaps not surprisingly, that relatively little of it found its way to the official owners. Salvors were offered enough of the food to ensure they were nourished throughout the working day, but clearly some interpreted this to mean they could take ashore whatever they could carry. As well as being heavily laden, others went home wearing four vests and three pullovers. Police searches were made and a number of prosecutions ensued but not all were successful. At Margate one boatman was seen wheeling a pram full of food around the streets while Police searched his house. A Dover man recalled how when he visited the pubs in the town he often fancied a cheese sandwich but all that he could get were filled with ham or turkey.

The exploitation of this wreck did not stop at its cargo. Several boatmen had loaded their boat with a number of brass scuttles and other non-ferrous metal components from the ship itself and were heading for a destination slightly further afield than the official landing point at Dover for salvaged material. Suddenly a Dover Harbour Board patrol boat was seen approaching them. Urging their motor to produce every last knot they tried to avoid the approaching launch but they could not and so, with extreme reluctance, the 'cargo' was surreptitiously thrown over the side. As the launch drew alongside a voice hailed, 'I'm not sure what you are up to, but young Tom's (one of the salvors) mum has been taken queer and so you'd better get back.'

Eventually the two halves of the *Helena Modjeska* were refloated and towed away to be scrapped. This was one rare occasion when a wreck survived long enough for all the cargo and the two parts of the hull to be recovered, one reason being that it had gone ashore in Trinity Bay on the inside of the Sands, but it was still very unusual. A whole ship and her freight of similar size could almost completely disappear in about two days on the off-side of the Goodwins.

The East Kent Coast.

A notable event in the early days of the lifeboats was the rescue of the crew of the American sailing ship *Northern Belle* after it had been driven ashore at Kingsgate, near Broadstairs, on 5 January 1857. On this occasion it was the two privately provided Broadstairs lifeboats *Mary White* and *Culmer White* which put off directly into a head sea to reach the wreck. The distance was not great but the height of the seas breaking on the rocks left all but the bravest seamen unmoved. While the lifeboatmen waited their chance to launch they reflected upon the fact that the Margate lugger *Victory* had already been sunk with the loss of all nine hands while trying to give help. Both boats had to be pulled out through this surf, requiring the crews to be changed after the first trip as some of the men were completely exhausted. Eventually all of the crew of the American vessel was brought safely ashore.

In terms of human endurance, most credit must, however, go to the men of the ship *Indian Chief* and the crew of the Ramsgate lifeboat *Bradford* towed by the steam tug *Vulcan* that rescued them on 5-6 January 1881 from the clutches of the Long Sand. This is really a north Kent wreck, but it is included here because of the location of the lifeboat which carried out the heroic rescue. In its execution both tug and open lifeboat spent twenty-six hours at sea in incredible conditions a long way from land. As the *Indian Chief* showed no distress signals, the tug and lifeboat had to lie hove to for most of the night until the wildest of dawns revealed 'the spider's line' of a mast in the chaotic maelstrom which was the Long Sand. It is difficult even to imagine the icy wind and lashing spray these men endured. On reaching the vessel the lifeboatmen found that seventeen of the crew of the *Indian Chief* had already perished and a further man died shortly after they got him into the boat. Incredibly, the remaining eleven were brought safely back to Ramsgate. Afterwards Coxswain Charles Fish, of the Ramsgate lifeboat, received the Institution's Gold Medal and his eleven colleagues each received the Silver Medal. Master Alf Page and his six crew of the tug *Vulcan* also received Silver Medals from the RNLI for one of the greatest services by any of their lifeboats.

A famous ship that remained visible for a long time was the German five-masted ship *Preussen*, one of the largest sailing vessels in the world when it was wrecked at Fan Bay, near South Foreland in 1910. A victim of a collision with a Newhaven-Dieppe cross-Channel steamer, the *Preussen* attempted to anchor under the lee of Dungeness. In the heavy weather prevailing she unfortunately lost both anchors and, the Dover tugs being unable to hold her, she drifted ashore under Langdon

Cliffs. All attempts to release her failed and once more the salvaged cargo was brought ashore. Some of it came up by the cliff hoist that was used to bring seaweed up from the beach. Whether this was an officially approved route is not known.

The Fan Bay area has attracted a number of victims over the years. In October 1926, the *Falcon*, a General Steam vessel trading between London and the continent sailed from Ostend carrying jute, cotton reels and a large quantity of matches in its cargo. On the voyage a fire started which rapidly enveloped the entire vessel. A tug's crew had earlier been able to place a towline aboard but the conflagration, fanned by the wind, caused this to burn through and the blazing hulk eventually drifted in under the cliffs at Langdon Steps where it burned out. South Foreland was the resting place of HMS *Nubian* in the First World War after a battle of the Dover Patrol. It was also the scene of the grounding of the largest ship ever to go ashore on the eastern coast of Kent. In 1952, on 13 January, the 17,700 gross-ton Panamanian oil tanker *Sovac Radiant* drove ashore there in a gale. Fortunately, she was unladen and after several attempts was refloated by tugs but she had sustained severe bottom damage. On this same day the French steamer *Agen* drove on to the Goodwins and broke in two.

Moving down to that part of the Kent coast between Dover and Dungeness, wrecks have been slightly less frequent. The most serious over the last two centuries has been the loss of the 951-ton sailing ship *Northfleet* off Dungeness on 22 January 1873. This vessel was run down while at anchor by a Spanish ship, the *Murillo*, which left the scene without waiting to assess the damage it had caused. At first this was not believed to be serious but a panic ensued when the *Northfleet* was found to be sinking and, despite limited help from other vessels, 320 of the 379 aboard were drowned. The *Murillo* was arrested eight months later and sold by order of a Court of Admiralty.

A further serious event was the sinking, on 31 May 1878, of the German ironclad *Grosser Kurfurst* following collision with a similar vessel the *Konig Wilhelm*, while trying to avoid sailing vessels off Folkestone. Considerable confusion in the collision avoidance procedure led to this tragic event which occurred in clear weather with a calm sea. In spite of this, 284 officers and men were lost from the *Grosser Kurfurst*, the survivors being picked up by the *Konig Wilhelm* and a third ironclad, the *Preussen*.

There are a number of cases of sailing ships breaking away from tugs and getting into difficulties in bad weather. One example was the *Benvenue* that drove ashore near Folkestone in hurricane conditions on 11 November 1891. The ship struck the bottom and settled down with the masts above water about 300 yards from the shore at Seabrook. In a situation somewhat reminiscent of the *Northern Belle*, local lifeboats made several unsuccessful attempts at launching. One resulted in the capsize of the Hythe lifeboat *Mayer de Rothschild* and the drowning of crew member Charles Fogg. In the end it was the bruised and battered coxswain Laurence Hennesey and the Hythe boat that rescued the twenty-seven survivors from the sailing ship, the master and four hands having already been lost. Coxswain Hennessey was awarded a well-deserved RNLI Silver Medal for this service.

In conclusion of this brief sketch of Kent shipwrecks it should be emphasised that, although there have been a number of tragic wrecks, these have been relatively few given the large period of time that is covered. Undoubtedly there have been a number of smaller vessels where the entire crew has been lost but, from the overall picture it appears that, despite frightful weather and the hazards of the sandbanks, many seafarers have survived shipwrecks, sometimes from what appear to be hopeless conditions. Obviously lifeboats have added greatly to the survival rate during the past 150 years.

As a final illustration, there occurred in 1971 a most unusual chain of events which determined the pattern for English Channel traffic separation that is observed today. In January of that year the Panamanian tanker *Texaco Caribbean* was on passage down Channel off the Varne Bank when she collided with a Peruvian vessel, the *Paracas*. A massive explosion occurred which blew the tanker apart, the bow sinking immediately and the stern remaining afloat for about twelve hours. The following day, a German ship, the *Brandenburg*, ran over the wreck and sank very quickly, with a consequent heavy loss of life. Many buoys were positioned at the site of the wrecks and a lightvessel, painted green, was also placed there. But still ships entered the wreck area or near-missed the manned lightvessel, until 27 February, when a Greek vessel, the *Niki*, ran over the wrecks and foundered with all hands. Altogether, fifty-one lives were lost in these accidents.

Nowadays, collisions are still a cause of damage to ships but the effective separation of traffic resulting from the previous incident and supervision by the Coastguards at Dover has drastically reduced the number of incidents. Additionally, pilots are necessary for passages of the Thames estuary and the Medway and that whole area is covered by radar surveillance from Port Control, London. Shipwrecks can still occur and, man remaining fallible, will undoubtedly continue in spite of all the navigational aids which are now available, albeit less frequently than in some of the unquiet times related here. Equally, the weather at sea must also always remain a challenge, search as it will to find any weakness in a vessel, which, if not identified, can lead to another entry in the casualty reports.

Kent Lifeboats to the Rescue.

Prior to the design of specially adapted craft for lifesaving, luggers and smaller sailing craft attempted to rescue those in difficulties at sea and were often successful. The Margate lugger *Lord Nelson* manned by a crew of seventeen managed to rescue 129 of the 143 aboard the *Hindostan* referred to earlier. Although early lifeboats such as that developed by Lionel Lukin were evaluated in the south-east they were not readily accepted. Lukin, the inventor of 'the unimmergible boat' in 1785 had it tested on the Kent coast. Although successful, it was subsequently lost or stolen and he did not pursue the subject a great deal further, leaving it to Henry Greathead to continue the development of the lifeboat. It is believed that a boat of his design was installed at Ramsgate in about 1802 but nothing is known about its activities.

Even though Sir William Hillary established the Lifeboat Institution in 1824, it was to be the middle of the century before boats dedicated to the saving of life at sea were entertained as a serious proposition in Kent. Lifeboats are mentioned for Dungeness in 1826, Dover from 1837 and a privately donated boat had reached Broadstairs by 1851. It was the *Northumberland* prize boat, however, which arrived at Ramsgate in 1852, with the availability of the harbour steam tug, that made it possible to rescue men in what had previously been considered impossible conditions. After this date other seaside towns rapidly introduced the following RNLI lifeboats: Margate (Private lifeboats 1857, RNLI boat 1860), North Deal (1863), Walmer (1856), Kingsdown (1866), Dover (1864), Folkestone, and Hythe (1876). Broadstairs lifeboat station closed in 1912. After motor lifeboats were introduced in the 1920s, the number of stations was further reduced as also was the number of men in the crews which went from typically fifteen, in a large pulling and sailing boat, to seven in the motorised version. Kingsdown closed in January 1927 and North Deal in 1932. Hythe was a victim of the Second World War.

Margate suffered the worst disaster to a Kent lifeboat in October 1897, when the boatmen's surfboat *Friend to all Nations* capsized shortly after launching in darkness to the sailing ship *Persian Empire*, reported to have been in collision. Nine of the crew, including the Coxswain William Cook, were drowned. It was an event which moved the nation and a very large amount of money was received by way of public donations, although relatively little of this reached the dependants of those who were lost. A lot was spent on a large marble monument for the communal grave and a statue for the seafront.

There were also a number of isolated single fatalities among the lifeboatmen at most of the stations, often due to exposure or the extreme effort required under the worst conditions. On some occasions the boatmen must have realised it was a gamble whether they would return safely or not. Beyond the need to save life, the prospect of a salvage award if the ship or cargo could be saved provided an extra incentive for boatmen whose incomes were insecure at the best of times.

Numerous acts of bravery have been observed or have gone unrecorded during the many rescues on the Kent coast in peace and war. Charles Fish of Ramsgate received three Gold Medals for his actions while coxswain of the Ramsgate Lifeboat. Fred Upton of *Walmer* was awarded two Silver Medals for rescues from Goodwins victims in the immediate post-war period of 1946-1952. So many have received medals of all kinds that it is difficult to single out any others for particular mention. Certainly there existed in profusion in the nineteenth century a breed of 'iron men,' who could endure extreme conditions at sea and who would not flinch in the face of danger.

One
The North Kent Coast

The infamous 1944 wreck of the 'Liberty' ship *Richard Montgomery* lies at the entrance to the River Medway about two miles from Garrison Point. It is highly respected for the 4,000 tons of bombs it still contains but after more than half a century the chance of explosion must be remote. It is the only relatively intact wreck visible on the Kent coast and its appearance changes with the weather, varying from threatening to benign.

Strandings were frequent further eastward along the Kent coast as shown in this print from Sharpe's *London Magazine* of 1849. These East Indiamen, the *Claudine* and *Westminster*, were apparently driven ashore at Margate to escape their loss in a gale. Both vessels later got off and resumed their service in the India trade. Others like the *Active* and *Hindostan* were not so lucky.

The wreck of the *Northern Belle* at Kingsgate near Margate early in 1857 was one of the first major rescues on the Kent coast involving lifeboats. All of those aboard the American sailing vessel were rescued by the Broadstairs lifeboats but the Margate lugger *Ocean* and her crew of nine was lost. Above is shown the two faces of the medal presented to the rescuers by the US Ambassador. In this case the recipient was Jethrow Miller of Broadstairs. Those lost from the *Ocean* were: John Smith, William Emptage, Isaac Solly, Abraham Busbridge, Charles Fuller, John Emptage, George Smith, Henry Paramor and Frederick Bath.

The loss of the 2,800-ton steamer *Deutschland* on the Kentish Knock in December 1875 illustrated the problem of communication with the shore when a casualty occurred on a remote sandbank in wintertime. Only nine years old, this vessel still sustained considerable losses among passengers and crew.

Strong north-easterly winds posed grave problems to sailing vessels anchored in Margate Roads. After the great storm of November 1877 the foreshore at Margate was littered with vessels, most of which were salved, except the *Charles Davenport* which had crashed through the shore end of the jetty and broken up.

Above all, the sinking of the paddle steamer *Princess Alice* after a collision in the sheltered waters of the Thames on 3 September 1878 was a pleasure steamer disaster of 'Titanic' proportions. This contemporary engraving shows the collier *Bywell Castle* striking the pleasure vessel a blow that virtually cut it in half.

About 640 passengers were lost from the crowded vessel that had almost completed a day's down river excursion in beautiful weather. The disaster occurred at the eastern end of Gallions Reach at Tripcock Point, or Margaret Ness, as it is better known. Recovery of the bodies was made more unpleasant by the extent of pollution of the river at that time.

An unknown schooner has driven ashore on the north Kent chalk ledges. Her fate is not known. Such vessels were sometimes so badly damaged that they could not be saved and were broken up where they lay. This was the fate of the schooner *Valkyr* that grounded at Birchington in 1919. Margate boatmen helped in the demolition of the vessel.

The Margate men helping to break up the *Valkyr* are, from left to right, front row: Harry Parker, Charles Epps, 'Sugar' Dixon, J. Gilbert, John 'Blossom' Taylor, William Mackie. Back row: 'Kitty' Hyde, Ted Parker, 'Roker' Mackie, Charlie 'Dusty' Miller, Jack Letley.

Quite large ships stranded on the Margate foreshore at times, an example being the Norwegian steamer *Coronel* which took the ground at Foreness in 1907. She was later successfully refloated with help from the Ramsgate tug *Aid*.

Pleasure craft were often not so lucky. The cabin cruiser *Collette* lies wrecked near the spot where the *Coronel* had grounded sixty years earlier.

Oil cargoes have always been dangerous and that in barrels aboard the barque *Blengfell* was no exception. The ship caught fire off Margate and was completely burnt out in October 1898 as depicted here by the *Illustrated London News*.

One of another group of vessels driven ashore, the Admiralty minesweeper *Yarmouth II*, lies at Ledge Point between Margate and Westgate on 20 September 1914. She was a trawler requisitioned for minesweeping duties.

Two major naval disasters occurred in the River Medway during the First World War. The 15,000-ton battleship HMS *Bulwark* was destroyed by one single huge explosion on 26 November 1914 which claimed ultimately 729 lives from her crew, there being only twelve survivors. Sheerness artist H.J. Snelling made this contemporary painting.

Only six months later, the minelayer *Princess Irene*, shown here in another work by H.J. Snelling, blew up in an enormous explosion in Saltpan Reach. More than two hundred of her crew and over seventy Sheerness Dockyard personnel were lost, there being only one survivor, stoker Ronald Wills.

The war may have ceased, but the north-east winds did not. Crowds mill around the SS *Dunvegan*, ashore just east of Margate jetty in April 1919. She settled across a stone groyne but the damage incurred was repaired after she was refloated.

Colliers were frequent callers at Margate, their cargoes destined for the local gasworks. This motor vessel, Everard's *Aqueity*, was driven past the harbour and ended up on Nayland Rock for Christmas 1938. The coal that was thrown overboard to lighten her was a welcome present to the local inhabitants. They arrived with prams, wheelbarrows and shopping bags to collect it.

Another steam coaster, the *Orchis*, was left high and dry at Foreness Point in March 1934. She was also safely recovered.

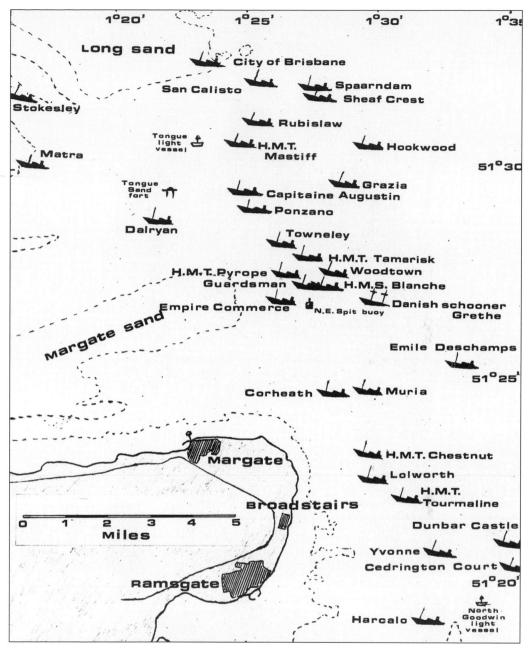

At the start of the Second World War the Germans laid many mines in the estuary. This chart shows the approximate positions of ships sunk due to enemy action off Margate during the Second World War. Almost all succumbed to magnetic mines.

The Eagle Oil tanker *San Calisto* sank after striking two mines off Margate.

Also going down by the bow is the small freighter *Sheaf Crest* which sank after striking a mine on 30 November 1939.

SS *Dalryan* had come all the way from the Pacific island of Nauru with fertiliser before being sunk off Margate.

The 4,500-ton *Dalryan* voyaging in peacetime before the war. She was a typical tramping freighter of which so many were to be lost in the war at sea of 1939-1945.

Margate lifeboat brings survivors from the SS *Dalryan* into the harbour on 1 December 1939. All were very pleased to reach the shore and grateful that hardly any injuries had been sustained. Not having any radio communication with the shore the lifeboat flew a red flag forward if it had casualties aboard.

At the sight of the flag a doctor and ambulance would be called to attend those like this seriously injured man brought ashore from the lost minesweeper HMS *Mastiff*.

While crowds look on, an ambulance travels along Margate jetty with men from the *Mastiff*. Such an event became commonplace in the autumn of 1939 and spring of 1940. Later crashed pilots were picked up and brought ashore.

If it did not kill outright, the massive explosion caused by a magnetic mine caused grave injuries to men aboard the ships that detonated them. Those who got 'the hammer' were often many months before they could go back to sea again. Here an injured man is landed from the SS *Woodtown*, which lost eight of her twelve crew.

In the midst of the mining campaign the Margate lifeboat was called out to a sunken sailing vessel, the Danish schooner *Grethe*. It was an eerie sight to see the sails set while the hull lay fathoms down. In fact she had earlier struck the Goodwins and no German device was responsible.

The Ellerman liner *City of Brisbane* became another wartime wreck when attacked by German aircraft and set on fire on 2 August 1940. The 8,000-ton ship drifted on to the South Long Sand where it was completely gutted. In spite of this, it remained a subject of further air attacks for some time.

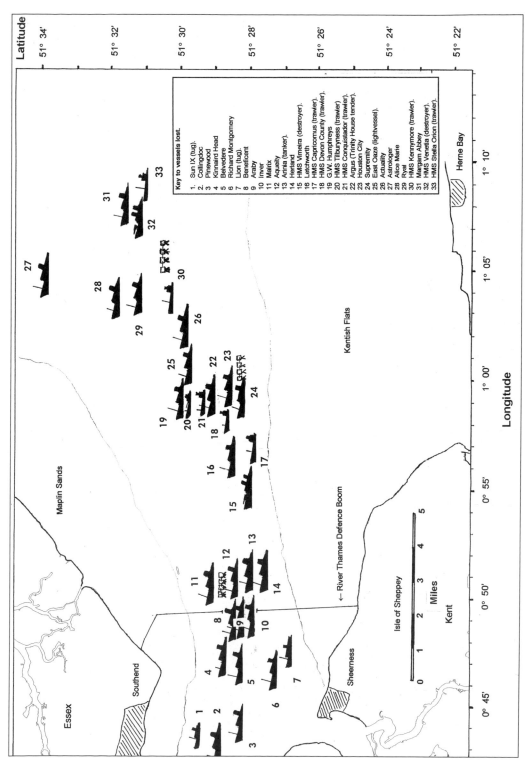

Latitude
Longitude

51° 34'
51° 32'
51° 30'
51° 28'
51° 26'
51° 24'
51° 22'

Key to vessels lost.

1. Sun IX (tug).
2. Collingdoc
3. Pinewood
4. Kinnaird Head
5. Belvedere
6. Richard Montgomery
7. Lion (tug).
8. Beneficent
9. Araby
10. Inver
11. Matrix
12. Aquety
13. Arinia (tanker).
14. Herland
15. HMS Vimeira (destroyer).
16. Letchworth
17. HMS Capricornus (trawler).
18. HMS Devon County (trawler).
19. G.W. Humphreys
20. HMS Tilburyness (trawler)
21. HMS Conquistador (trawler).
22. Argus (Trinity House tender).
23. Houston City
24. Supremity
25. East Gaze (lightvessel).
26. Actuality
27. Astrologer
28. Alice Marie
29. Ryal
30. HMS Kennymore (trawler).
31. Margam Abbey
32. HMS Venetia (destroyer).
33. HMS Stella Orion (trawler).

Maplin Sands

Essex

Southend

Kentish Flats

← River Thames Defence Boom

Sheerness

Isle of Sheppey

Kent

Herne Bay

Miles
0 1 2 3 4 5

A chart of vessels lost off Sheerness and Southend due to enemy action during the Second World War. Again nearly all of them were sunk by mines.

A daily user of the river, the London County Council sludge carrier *G.W. Humphreys* was one of four built in the 1920s. She was mined in the East Oaze Deep in October 1940 and sank with the loss of seven of her crew. This painting by T.W. Jay is on display at the Crossness Pumping Station Museum.

HM Submarine *Truculent* and sixty-four Naval and Chatham Dockyard personnel were lost due to collision with a Swedish tanker in the Medway approaches in January 1950.

Later many vessels, including local lifeboats, searched for survivors but few were found. The destroyer HMS *Cowdray* acted as a command vessel for search activities.

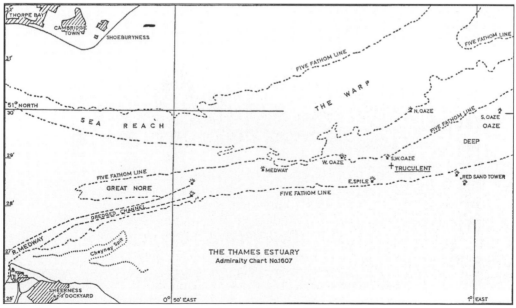

This chart shows the approximate position of sinking of HMS *Truculent*.

One vessel that almost became a wreck. The famous four-masted sail training ship *Pamir* dragged her anchor near the Kentish Knock in January 1952 during a severe gale. After the Margate and Walton lifeboats had stood by her for many hours a slight improvement in the weather enabled the ship to slip her anchor and clear the sands. The *Pamir* was later lost in a hurricane off the Azores.

An elegant auxiliary schooner now lying derelict, the *Hans Egede* was a victim of fire off the Dutch coast in August 1955. She was towed to Dover where the local Fire Brigade extinguished the fire. There was a proposal to convert her into a sail training ship but nothing came of this and, around 1962, she was beached near Cliffe jetty on the Thames, where she has been allowed to fall to pieces.

Regular coal cargoes continued to arrive at Margate up until May 1958. In December of the previous year another one went slightly astray when the MV *Continuity* missed the entrance channel and ended up on the Marine sands.

Working in close proximity with ships meant that berthing tugs were occasionally overtaken by disaster when they could not avoid a collision with the vessel they were assisting. William Watkins' tug *Kenia* was a victim of such an event when she was undocking the *Maashaven* from Tilbury Dock in October 1964.

On 27 October 1964 the East German vessel *Magdeburg*, carrying a deck cargo of buses for Cuba, was in collision with the inward-bound Japanese vessel *Yamashiro Maru*, off Broadness Point, Northfleet. Left in a sinking condition, the *Magdeburg* was rapidly beached at Broadness but quickly rolled over on to her side. Fortunately all fifty-six aboard were saved by tugs that rushed to her assistance. Eventually she was raised and made seaworthy but was lost later while under tow in the Bay of Biscay.

A more modern effluent carrier, the year-old Sir Joseph Rawlinson, was also lost in the Oaze Deep after collision with a hopper barge under tow in September 1965. The ship capsized and sank rapidly, taking nine men down with her. About a year later she was raised and towed to London.

Occasionally, very large vessels have grounded in the Thames. The 97,000-gross ton *Olympic Athlete* was one of the biggest: she went ashore on 17 February 1972 near the oil refinery jetty where she was intended to berth. Although never in any serious danger, the tanker did block the river for a time and six tugs were needed to move her.

Small ships more often found themselves in difficulties. In July 1972, the master of the German vessel *Rustringen* found her hold flooding off Margate and beached her on the Margate Sand to prevent her sinking. Later tugs endeavoured to get her to London, but she sank. Her remains were eventually raised and broken up near Tilbury Fort.

On 27 October 1997 the gravel dredger *Sand Kite* struck one of the concrete piers of the Thames Barrier and sank. A combined operation between the Port of London Authority and Howard Smith's tugs ensured that the ship was quickly raised and removed. Later the *Sand Kite* was repaired and returned to service.

A very recent wreck on the Thames was that of another dredger, the *Arco Arun*, which struck the bottom and later capsized in Northfleet Hope in October 1998. It sank in almost an identical position to the *Magdeburg* in 1964. The *Arco Arun* was eventually righted and refloated by the same method as used for the East German vessel.

Two
The Goodwin Sands

Wreckers by reputation, but firm to walk upon at low tide, the Goodwins have been the venue for various sporting activities over the years. Stretching in total for some ten miles from north-east to south-west and situated about five miles from the shore, they give an overwhelming impression of isolation and desolation.

The Great Storm of 20 November 1703 is regarded as the worst in recorded history. Four major Naval ships, the *Restoration*, *Stirling Castle*, *Northumberland* and *Mary*, were all lost in the turmoil surrounding the Goodwin Sands and nearer to twenty merchant ships were also cast away and sunk. Some idea of the chaos is shown in this engraving of a somewhat later date.

The conditions faced by the sailors afloat on that dreadful night in 1703 are hard to describe. There was only one survivor from the *Mary* and about eighty from the *Stirling Castle*, whose end can be imagined from this engraving. It is believed that a number of men landed on the Goodwins, but that only delayed their ultimate fate.

One of the most famous wrecks on the Goodwins in more recent times was that of the Brocklebank steamer *Mahratta* in 1909, partly because another *Mahratta* joined her thirty years later. Here the ship has already broken in two on the sandbank.

A closer view of the broadside of the vessel while salvage of the tea cargo was being undertaken.

The heavy list of the SS *Mahratta* is apparent when seen from aft.

Salvage work in progress aboard the wrecked ship. Men suffered anxious moments if a ship started to break up under their feet.

Seen here in service pre-war, the second *Mahratta* was built in 1917 and wrecked on the Goodwins in October 1939.

A sad end awaits the *Mahratta* (II). Less cargo was salvaged from this wreck than from the earlier vessel, partly due to wartime conditions and also the greater speed with which she broke up.

The Belgian freighter *Kabinda* was another vessel that broke in two while salvage work was being attempted. Ramsgate and Walmer lifeboats had to rush to the rescue of the men involved in December 1939.

A second Belgian steamer, the *Flandres*, was sunk by collision in the Downs with the *Kabalo*, a sister of the Kabinda, on 12 February 1940.

A further victim of the Goodwins unconnected with hostilities was the collier *Ashley* which was lost on the northern end of the sands on 9 March 1940.

All that remained of the *Ashley* about a year after her stranding. As the Goodwins lightships had been sunk or removed and there was considerable congestion of shipping in the area, losses on the Sands became frequent.

Immediately after the war there was a spate of Goodwins wrecks, generally due to the masters of American vessels not requesting pilots or taking due care in their navigation. The 'Victory' ship SS *Luray Victory* struck the off-side of the sands at the southern end on 30 January 1946.

The 7,600-ton *Luray Victory* broke up rapidly, causing her holds to flood and therefore very little of her cargo was saved.

44

A sister vessel, the *Northeastern Victory*, followed suit on Christmas Eve 1946. She also foundered rapidly but, like the *Luray Victory*, her masts and derricks remained clearly visible from Deal for many years.

Northeastern Victory when seen from the air reveals her sunken hull.

In between these events there occurred the infamous stranding of an American 'Liberty,' the *Helena Modjeska*. This vessel, which had previously been anchored in the Downs, went ashore on the Goodwins after leaving Trinity Bay bound northward on 12 September 1946. About three days later the ship broke in two. Salvage work proved difficult in view of her complex cargo.

While efforts were being made to refloat the *Helena Modjeska*, the SS *Fort Vermillion*, carrying a cargo of iron ore, went ashore quite close to her in fog. There were fears that she might also become a wreck. However, after seven days of intensive effort, she was safely removed from the sands.

The wreck of the *Helena Modjeska* became a tourist attraction. Boat trips were offered from local ports to take sightseers out to the Goodwins for a closer examination.

There were numerous lorries aboard, mostly carried as deck cargo. These were loaded on to a hired landing craft and taken to Dover and Deal. Salvage men were paid six shillings an hour, which included danger money.

Large pieces of road building equipment were also stowed on the deck. Here a mobile crane is being unloaded into the landing craft LCT 723. The great quantity and variety of the deck cargo is apparent.

Einar Backmann, American Chief Engineer of the *Helena Modjeska*, remained with the ship to supervise the salvage work after her captain had been found dead in his hotel room at Ramsgate.

During the course of the salvage, the weather and the tide moved the two parts of the ship about in relation to each other. Much of the deck cargo remaining on the after section is visible here.

Less than three months after the wrecking of the *Northeastern Victory* a Greek 'Liberty' ship, the *Ira*, laden with coal, ran aground very close to the *Luray Victory* and once more broke in half. Walmer lifeboat rescued thirty-four from this casualty.

A mast of the *Ira* appears in the distance between the after king posts and derricks of the *Luray Victory*. These frequent wrecks gained for the southern Goodwins the name of 'Calamity Corner'.

On 2 January 1948 the Italian steamer *Silvia Onorato* went ashore almost due west of the East Goodwin lightship. Coxswain Freddie Upton was awarded the RNLI Silver Medal for the rescue of the thirty crew members and the captain's dog.

Master of the *Silvia Onorato* was fifty-two-year-old Captain Francesco Ruocco.

A later aerial view of the *Silvia Onorato* shows how the later Goodwins wrecks nearly always broke amidships.

Close to finally disappearing, the wreck of the *Silvia Onorato* demonstrates graphically how the bow and stern of a stranded vessel would sink while the amidships section remained supported.

Four lightvessels eventually marked the Goodwin Sands. They were identified as North Goodwin, Gull, East Goodwin and South Goodwin. All four were painted red and showed distinctive lights at night. In spite of this they were frequently victims of collisions. In March 1929 the Gull lightvessel was rammed and sunk by the Ellerman liner *City of York*. The master was drowned but the other six crew luckily escaped.

In July 1929 the Gull lightvessel was raised and brought to Ramsgate for examination and temporary repair. Later it was fully refitted, given a new name and placed in a less vulnerable position near the Brake Sand.

There was always the possibility that a lightvessel might break adrift. While they were manned the emergency bower anchors could always be let go. After the Second World War commenced, the crews were gradually withdrawn due to the frequency of enemy air attacks upon them. While unmanned, the North Goodwin lightship broke away and drove ashore at Walmer in October 1940, amid the beach defences.

One of the most tragic wrecks on the Goodwins in the twentieth century was that of the South Goodwin lightvessel, lost in November 1954 with all of her crew; only a birdwatcher survived. A similar event to that described previously, the vessel broke adrift in hurricane conditions and struck the sands she was intended to guard, capsized completely and became overwhelmed by the heavy seas.

South Goodwin Lightvessel No.90 moored on station to the south of the Sands before her loss. Intended to warn ships of the dangerous shoals, she became a victim herself.

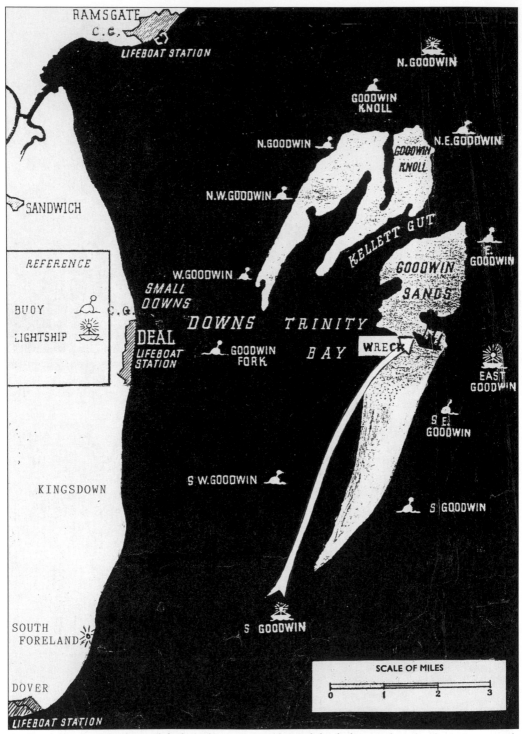

A chart showing the line of drift and position of loss of the lightvessel, only about forty yards from the far side of the sands. No trace of her crew was ever found.

56

At low tide Ronald Murton, a representative of the Ministry of Agriculture and Fisheries, was lifted to safety by a US Air Force helicopter from Manston airfield. It was one of the first air-sea rescues to take place and the pilot Curtis F. Parkins received a Silver Medal from the RNLI for his efforts.

A few remains of the South Goodwin lightvessel were still visible in 1994. On a calm summer day two lifeboat davits projected from the sand as a solemn reminder of the tragic event of forty years previously.

A further example of the danger of the Goodwin Sands. A chance examination by an RAF helicopter in bad weather found the catamaran *Aku-Aku* breaking up on the sandbank. Her crew was in a desperate situation.

In a last minute rescue from almost certain drowning, the occupants of the *Aku-Aku* were winched aboard the helicopter and taken to Manston aerodrome. These dramatic pictures were taken by Margate photographer Chris Fright.

Three
The East Kent Coast

St. Margaret's Bay and the South Foreland have also attracted their share of casualties. This sailing vessel, the *Firth of Cromarty*, became stranded in the former in 1894. After removal of most of her cement cargo the ship was successfully refloated and taken to Dover.

The barque *Vega* lies ashore at Deal, *c*.1880. One of many that over the years graced the shingle beach, the absence of rocks meant that such ships often survived grounding here as well as on the north coast.

Dungeness, the southernmost part of Kent, has had its fair share of disasters, one of the most memorable being the loss of the sailing vessel *Northfleet* on 22 January 1873. Run into by the Spanish ship *Murillo* while at anchor, the vessel sank quickly.

In an attempt to quell the panic that occurred when his ship sank the master of the *Northfleet* raised his pistol, but this was to little avail for 320 persons were lost of the 379 aboard.

Most famous of the wrecks near the South Foreland was that of the *Preussen*, wrecked in Fan Bay in 1910. This five-masted ship was one of the largest of her day.

The *Preussen* suffered a collision with the Newhaven-Dieppe Channel steamer *Brighton* and was forced to return up channel due to damage to her bows and deteriorating weather. Having lost both anchors off Dungeness and become unmanageable, she later drove ashore near South Foreland lighthouse on 7 November 1910.

Seen with the white cliffs in the background, the damage sustained to her bowsprit and foremast as a result of the collision is apparent. However, all crew and passengers of the *Preussen* were saved.

When seen from the deck, the masts and rigging of the *Preussen* made an impressive sight.

At first, there were hopes that the huge vessel would be refloated, but these were unfortunately not realised and the *Preussen* was gradually broken up where she lay.

The hull of the *Preussen* remained visible until well after the First World War. By that time she was nothing more than a sad relic of a once proud ship. At very low tides her ribs and bottom plates can still be seen to this day.

Although the ship has very largely disappeared, some of her cargo has survived, including these china plates which were part of the contents of a crate that Henry George Curling brought up by the seaweed hoist at Langdon Cliffs.

Laeisz's Flying 'P' ships were very unlucky in respect of collisions for in March 1912, almost two years after the *Preussen* was lost, the *Pisagua* was in collision with the P&O liner *Oceana* off Eastbourne. This time it was the steamer which sank but the *Pisagua* was very lucky to survive, her damage if anything being greater than that of the *Preussen*. Only the fine weather saved her. She is seen here after being brought into Dover.

Wartime mining victims were just as frequent off the east part of Kent as they were in the Thames. The largest vessel to be lost in this way off the Kent shore was the 10,000-ton Union-Castle intermediate liner *Dunbar Castle*, seen here in peacetime.

While travelling in convoy, the *Dunbar Castle* foundered off the North Foreland on 9 January 1940, her upperworks remaining above water. Her master was killed by the foremast falling on to the bridge. The wreck was not dispersed until after the war.

Another casualty of the magnetic mine was the Norwegian steamer *Bravore*, which sank four miles off Ramsgate in April 1940. Four injured survivors were recovered but fourteen other crew members and four French Naval ratings were lost.

In the case of the General Steam Navigation cargo vessel *Merel*, here seen near Tower Bridge, the losses were similar, sixteen being killed out of her crew of eighteen when she was sunk on 8 December 1939.

Pleasure piers were deliberately cut off from the shore at a number of towns to prevent invaders arriving by that route. At Deal that work was not necessary as a previously mined Dutch coaster, the *Nora*, completed the task in January 1940. In bad weather the ship broke adrift and, with no power available, struck the pier.

Afterwards, a large hole was left in the pier and the *Nora* resided on the beach lying on her side.

Although access to the beach was limited, crowds gathered to see the damage to the pier and witness the fate of the *Nora*.

The later war years brought a further spate of collisions, some with dire consequences. In 1944 the 'Liberty' ship *James Harrod*, carrying cased petrol, caught fire after such an incident and burned for a long time. The ship later grounded at Walmer and broke in half. The wreck was the subject of salvage work over a long period and an explosion of the resulting cargo was the cause of the deaths of a number of men at the railway station.

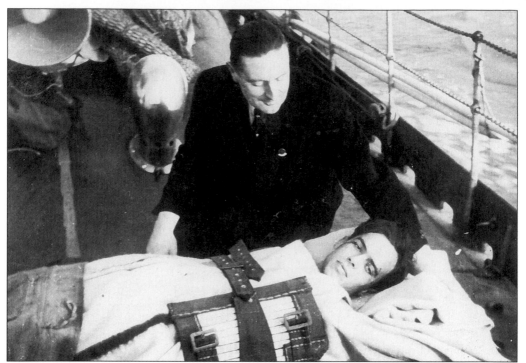

During the war and for a considerable period afterwards medical help was rendered to ill or injured men aboard vessels in the Downs by Dr. James Hall. Never deterred, even by the worst of weather, the 'Lifeboat Doctor' as he became known, treated many seafarers such as this stretcher case being brought ashore by the Walmer lifeboat.

Tugs were an important requirement for the successful salvage of large ships and William Watkins' *Rumania* was stationed at Dover in the 1950s in order to be immediately available if any accident occurred.

A winter casualty revealed at South Foreland. The Italian 'Liberty' ship *Monviso* lies aground in February 1955, with the tug *Rumania* in the background waiting to assist and the Dover lifeboat standing by. The *Monviso* was safely returned to her native element.

The lilac-painted ocean salvage tug *Rumania* was, however, lost on the Long Sand only a year later. In another nail-biting helicopter rescue, the last of the crew was literally taken off as the tug slipped beneath the waves.

Following pages: The largest vessel to run ashore at South Foreland and, for that matter, anywhere on the Kent coast east of Sheerness, was the Panamanian tanker *Sovac Radiant*, seen here under the cliffs on 13 January 1952. Six tugs refloated the vessel the next day. She was lucky, she could so easily have remained there, becoming a wreck like the *Preussen*, or suffered the fate of the *Agen*.

71

Wrecked on the Goodwins while the *Sovac Radiant* was immobilised at Fan Bay, the French vessel *Agen* quickly broke in two. Freddie Upton bravely took the Walmer lifeboat between the two halves of the ship to rescue the crew. Afterwards, her cargo of huge hardwood logs drifted about the Straits and became a hazard to shipping of another kind.

A popular place for wrecks, the beach between South Foreland and Dover Harbour was the final resting-place for the steamer *Falcon*, owned by the General Steam Navigation Company. On passage from Ostend to London in October 1926, the ship caught fire and, blazing from stem to stern, drifted ashore at Langdon Cliffs. Here is shown all that remained of the vessel in 1963. It appears to be very much the same today.

Once the Straits of Dover are reached, collisions become the main cause for concern. Here the Dutch MV *Prins Alexander* lies down by the head following contact with the Norwegian steamer NO *Rogenaes* in July 1952.

A Dover tug, the *Lady Duncannon*, towed the *Prins Alexander* into Dover Harbour.

The Dover Harbour Board tugs *Lady Brassey* and *Lady Duncannon* were maids of all work around the harbour, but they both additionally accomplished a considerable amount of salvage work during their working lives. *Lady Brassey*, easily distinguished by her twin funnels, served from 1913 to 1958.

Lady Duncannon bears the later Dover Harbour Board livery in this 1956 picture. Completed in 1914, the tug was sold to Cardiff in 1958 for further service.

Fortunately, collisions in the English Channel are now relatively rare, but one ship, the Norwegian MV *Hassel*, suffered two off Dover in little more than a year. On the first occasion, in May 1956, following a collision with a Liberian tanker, the vessel was beached at Seabrook, near Folkestone.

After repairs the *Hassel* sailed again but was brought into Dover once more in August 1957, cut down again on her starboard side after colliding with a French ship.

A very serious accident occurred in the shipping lane east of Dover on 9 June 1955, when the laden Swedish oil tanker *Johannishus* struck the Panamanian freighter *Buccaneer*. An explosion resulted and the tanker was almost immediately swept by fire.

The crew was forced to jump from the blazing ship, still moving ahead, into a sea that was rapidly becoming covered by fire. In such circumstances it is surprising that only twenty of the forty-two aboard lost their lives. The remainder were picked up by passing ships and most were transferred to the Margate pilot boat.

Later the survivors of the *Johannishus* were landed at Margate jetty.

No attempt could be made to board the *Johannishus* until the fire had subsided. Tugs waited by her for many hours. Although her superstructure was completely burnt out, amazingly the greater part of her oil cargo remained intact.

Extreme weather also took its toll on Channel shipping over the years. In July 1956 the British MV *Teeswood* capsized off Dungeness in hurricane force winds and later sank off Dover. Some survivors were picked up by the tanker BP Distributor and taken to Margate.

A first voyage survivor from MV *Teeswood* indicates his relief at being safely landed at Margate.

After the war, the Downs remained a place of refuge in the event of accident and to this haven the Pakistani steamship *Yousuf Baksh* was brought in May 1965, a fire having broken out in her jute cargo. The fire spread quickly and it was four days before it was extinguished, one fireman losing his life in the process. The ship was a total loss.

In August 1966, the Dutch coaster *Hunzeborg* was beached at Sandown near Deal for repairs following a collision in the Straits of Dover.

A further event of momentous proportions occurred in January 1971, when the Panamanian tanker *Texaco Caribbean* (above) was in collision with the Peruvian motor vessel *Paracas* two miles west of the Varne Bank.

An enormous explosion occurred which blew the tanker in half, her bow section sinking immediately and her stern section following about twelve hours later.

MV *Paracas* – the other ship involved in the collision. She suffered relatively little damage.

Next day the German vessel *Brandenburg* ran over the wreckage and sank within about five minutes. Her passing was unseen and therefore eleven of the thirty-two aboard were fortunate to be rescued.

Many buoys were laid at the wreck site and a lightvessel installed but, in spite of this, the Greek MV *Niki* also ran through the area on 27 February and sank with the loss of all twenty-two aboard.

One visible sign, the topmast of the MV *Niki*, shows as a cross above water, marking the graves of her crew. These wrecks, which in total cost more than fifty lives, provided the stimulus to bring into effect the traffic separation scheme which exists in the Straits of Dover today.

Returning to inshore waters, the tug *Neg Chieftain* capsized and sank off Ramsgate in August 1983 while towing a barge loaded with stone for the extension to the harbour. It was later raised by the floating sheerlegs *Taklift 1* and brought into Ramsgate in December 1984.

One vessel overcome by the hurricane of October 1987 was the cross-Channel ferry *Hengist*. Berthed in the harbour at Folkestone she started to break her moorings as the wind increased in violence. Her master decided to put to sea but, as the ship left harbour, the motion experienced shut down all power aboard her. As a consequence she drifted ashore at Copt Point, Folkestone. After about a month the ferry was refloated, repaired and put back into service.

The most recent of the English Channel collisions involved the 50,000-ton cruise ship *Norwegian Dream* and the container ship *Ever Decent*. In the very early hours of 24 August 1999 the cruise ship, which was returning to Dover from Norway with some 2,300 passengers and crew aboard, struck the *Ever Decent* off the Falls Bank about 20 miles north-east of Margate. The container ship had earlier left the River Medway heading for Zeebrugge. There were very few injured aboard the cruise liner, but the damage to the ship was severe, as can be seen in this picture of the ship after she arrived at Dover.

At the moment of the collision a fire broke out on board the 52,000-ton *Ever Decent*. Due to the flammable content of some of the containers it took five days for tugs with fire-fighting equipment to bring the blaze under control. The ships were in international waters when the collision occurred but, as the event could easily have been more serious, it had an impact on maritime authorities and public opinion right around the Kent coast. The *Ever Decent* eventually proceeded to her planned destination.

Four
Kentish Lifeboats
to the Rescue

The *Quiver*, Margate's first RNLI lifeboat, arrived in 1860 and remained there until 1883.

Margate

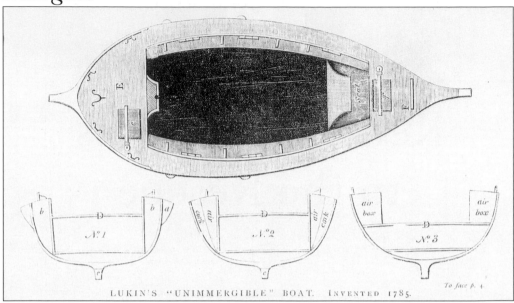

LUKIN'S "UNIMMERGIBLE" BOAT. INVENTED 1785.

Lionel Lukin's 'Unimmergible' boat invented in 1785 was tested on the Kent coast. Although he did not make great progress with his design, he is generally regarded as the inventor of the lifeboat. He is buried in the churchyard at Hythe.

The Margate lifeboat *Quiver* attending a vessel in distress in Margate Roads in February 1869. The *Lifeboat* journal reported: 'It blew a hurricane here on 12 February. About seven o'clock in the evening the schooner *Friends* of West Hartlepool went ashore near the jetty. The lifeboat went out to her through the very heavy sea then running, and was fortunately enabled to save the shipwrecked crew of five men, the boat, however, being somewhat damaged in performing the service. This engraving from the *Illustrated Times* portrays the incident more graphically than the simple statement above. There have been many such shipwrecks on the coast of Kent.

Air — "*Hearts of Oak.*"

Lines Written on the Occasion of

A GALLANT RESCUE

BY THE MARGATE LIFEBOAT "QUIVER,"

Of the crew of the brig "Sarah," of Sunderland, which was wrecked on the Margate Sands,
on the 25th January, 1871.

BY HARMAN KEBLE.

On a cold winter's night, and a still colder day,
An ill-fated brig on the *Margate Sands lay,
To her yards climb the men, leave her hull 'neath the wave,
And cry, in despair, is there no one to save?

CHORUS:—Trim and taut are our boats ; brave and true are our men,
For signals, look steady,
Now lads, make ready,
And with the storm we'll wrestle, on the main, on the main.

There ashore reels the ship, with her topsails all torn,
And captain and crew dread their fate so forlorn,
Who, for fifteen long hours, on the topmast and stay,
†All together pass the weary time away.

Their sad lot they mourn, and they anxiously peer
Through cold blinding sleet, O most dreadfully drear ;
To the north, to the south, east and west, all around
In vain they keep watch, for no help can be found.

The bleak night is o'er, and the grey morn appears,
And brings them fresh hopes, though they're mingled with fears.
Hey ! my lads ! now they cry, what is this on the lee ?
'Tis the Margate Lifeboat soon they plainly see.

ON THE MARGATE PIER.

O, wild blows the wind, and the waves with a roar,
'Gainst the "Quiver" roll as she bounds from the shore ;
On, on, she braves the storm, with sturdy men and true,
And back brings 'mid cheers the weather-beaten crew.

The "Quiver," one of the National Lifeboat Institution's boats, was manned by the following
Margate boatmen:—

*Coxswain—*WM. GRANT. *2nd Coxswain—*WM. JONES.

W. BROCKMAN.	A. EMPTAGE.	H. HARMAN.	J. TAYLOR.
R. BROCKMAN.	E. EMPTAGE.	S. LADD.	WM. PARKER.
W. COLLINS.	J. FOX.	G. SANDWELL.	

Let's honor, then, our lifeboat men,
Their gallant deeds extol ;
Remember, then, these thirteen men,
Each one of us and all.

Go, search the world, none shall be found
Possessed of hearts more true ;
As years roll round, praise shall resound
For this brave Margate crew.

* These dangerous Sands are situate about 5 miles N.W. of Margate.

" The Margate lugger 'Ocean' manned by W. Company, master, J. Epps, senr., J. Epps, junr., Joseph Epps, J. Knight, J. Walker, W. Parker, junr., W. Tucker, H. Jones, J. Jones, J. Emptage, H. Brockman, and T. Taylor, was promptly put to sea, her sails were hoisted with a merry cheer and amidst the blinding sleet and heavy sea steered to the rescue. But as soon as she neared the wreck it was found impossible through the breaking sea to approach sufficiently near to render assistance, and probably had it not been for the lesser draught of the life boat the shipwrecked crew must have been lost."
† " We took refuge," said one of the shipwrecked crew, " in the ' foretop ' after seeing our hopeless condition, and huddled ourselves together for warmth, cheering each other to hold on."—*Keble's Gazette.*

Marginal left (vertical): They were saved after great and heroic efforts on the part of the lifeboat's crew, W. S. Jones, the second coxswain, nearly losing his own life. As a memento, some friends presented him with a silver watch. As the lifeboat entered the Harbour, and drew alongside the stoneway near the Droit Office, it was seen that six half-frozen sailors had been rescued.

Marginal right (vertical): The Silver Medal of the Royal National Lifeboat Institution and a copy of its vote inscribed on vellum were presented to William Grant, 1st coxswain of the "Quiver" lifeboat together with £8 18s. to himself and crew in testimony of their gallant services.—A public subscription was also raised by the inhabitants in admiration of their conduct.

A ballad composed to celebrate the saving of the crew of the Sunderland brig *Sarah* that was wrecked on Margate Sands in 1871. Her crew also owed their rescue to the first *Quiver* lifeboat donated to Margate by the magazine of the same name.

The capsize of the Margate surfboat *Friend to All Nations* on 2 November 1897 was the worst lifeboat accident in Kent. Nine lives were lost including that of the coxswain, William Cook. Afterwards the boat was drawn up on the Parade, where it attracted much public attention.

Only four of the thirteen aboard the *Friend to All Nations* survived. They are, from left to right: Joe Epps, Henry Brockman, Robert Ladd and John Gilbert.

Huge crowds witnessed the funeral procession for the nine victims of the Margate surfboat disaster.

An impressive central feature, created out of Carrara marble, marked the communal grave for the lost lifeboatmen at the cemetery.

After the disaster to the Margate surfboat it was repaired and saw further use. About a year later, while being towed by a tug, the bow post was pulled out and the boat abandoned in a sinking condition. It was later washed ashore at Gorleston and taken to a local boatyard. Although subsequently returned to Margate, its life-saving days were over.

A Seamen's Institute with a reading room was constructed at Margate in 1865 for the benefit of the local boatmen. It also served as a lookout to give early warning of ships in distress and was used up until the 1930s.

The second *Quiver No.1* seen with her crew at about the time of the capsize of the *Friend to All Nations*. Most Lifeboat Institution boats of the time were self-righting but heavier, and they needed more horses and people to launch them.

Two slipway-launched boats, the *Eliza Harriett* and the *Civil Service No.1* replaced the *Quiver No.1*. Each was held by a chain at the top of a jetty slipway. Members of the local lifeboat committee and Coastguard launchers are seen standing in front of the *Eliza Harriett* in 1902. They are, from left to right: T. Brehont, Thomas Wallis, Chief Officer Dent, T.B. Jephcott and T. Jephcott (Honorary Secretary).

In Memoriam Of Three Margate Boatmen who were Drowned on Sunday, Nov. 8th, 1908, in the galley "Reindeer," off Margate.

LEWIS, PRINTERS, MARGATE

HERBERT PARKER,
AGED 27 YEARS.

WILLIAM PARKER,
AGED 42 YEARS.

JOHN EPPS,
AGED 32 YEARS.

Three Margate men were lost from the galley Reindeer in 1908. One of the Epps family was amongst those who died.

When a motor lifeboat was allocated to Margate a new boathouse was constructed on the eastern side of the jetty. The naming ceremony of *The Lord Southborough* (*Civil Service No.1*) took place at Margate in 1925.

The launching of *The Lord Southborough* seen from the top of the slipway. This boat saved a very large number of men from the wartime victims of the mines in the Thames estuary.

The boathouse constructed to house *The Lord Southborough* lasted from 1925 until it was partially destroyed by the 1978 storm, when the jetty connecting it to the shore collapsed. A year or so later the remainder was demolished.

William 'Paddy' Walker, well-known Margate fisherman and lifeboatman. An immensely strong swimmer, he once fell overboard from his sailing bawley while fishing alone, swam after it and reboarded it successfully.

THIS TESTIMONIAL together with a solid silver engraved watch, publicly subscribed for, was PRESENTED TO Skipper *W. Walker*, in recognition of his gallantry, when, comprising one of the crew of the Motor-Boat "*Thanet Queen*" on May 16ᵗʰ 1926, he set out in a very heavy sea and effected an heroic rescue of two lives from a small drifting boat.

A testimonial presented to 'Paddy' Walker for saving the two people aboard a craft which had drifted over from the Essex coast.

The crew of the Margate lifeboat assembled at the front of the boathouse in the later war period. They are, from left to right: Harry Sandwell, Mr Tatham (Harbourmaster), Edwin Jordan (Motor Mechanic), Harry Parker, Alf Lacey, Ted Parker (Coxswain), Arthur Ladd, Denis Price, Ted Parker Jnr.

Denis Price was coxswain of the lifeboat at Margate in the 1950s, when the *North Foreland* (*Civil Service No.11*) was there.

The lifeboat *North Foreland* arrives from the builders in 1951. She was later fitted with an enclosed cockpit and self-righting apparatus. The boat is currently on display at Chatham Historic Dockyard.

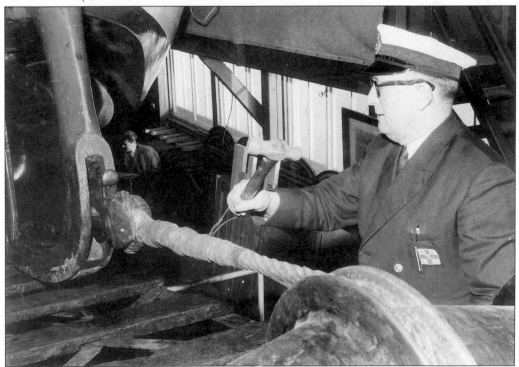

The Watson lifeboat *North Foreland* (*Civil Service No.11*) succeeded The *Lord Southborough*. She used the same boathouse and was launched in an identical way by striking the release hook with a hammer. George Wilson demonstrates the procedure.

Lifeboat motor mechanic Alf Lacey BEM uses the radio aboard the *North Foreland*. He joined the lifeboat in 1940 and became mechanic in 1947. When he retired, in 1981, he was the longest serving in that capacity in the RNLI.

The motor vessel *Lisbeth* M was carrying a cargo of stone when she collided with the Central Electricity Generating Board collier *Sir John Snell*. Because of her cargo, she sank very quickly.

Survivors from the *Lisbeth* M gather together after their ship was sunk by collision in fog off Margate in 1957.

A body of a crewman from the *Lisbeth* M is carried ashore.

Ramsgate

Isaac Jarman was coxswain of the
Ramsgate lifeboat from 1860 to 1870.

At Ramsgate the lifeboats lie always
afloat. This is the fourth *Bradford*, the
last of those to be donated by the City
of Bradford. Some lifeboatmen have
been known to swim out to the boats to
be sure of a place in the crew.

A lookout was always kept in bad weather at all the Kent ports with lifeboats.

33 RAMSGATE. — On the "Look Out". — LL.

The Ramsgate tug and lifeboat at sea, from a painting by H. Franklin & Son of Deal, entitled *A wreck on the Goodwin Sands*.

If a distressed vessel was sighted, or the lightvessels off the Goodwins fired their cannons to indicate that a ship was in trouble, a bell was rung to call the crew of the lifeboat. This was the case with the *Indian Chief*. Later maroons were used for this purpose.

An engraving of the lifeboat *Bradford* approaching a wreck. Although used to portray the *Indian* Chief service it was in fact created much earlier.

104

Charles Fish, was coxswain of the Ramsgate lifeboat at the time of the famous *Indian Chief* rescue. He went on to receive two more Gold Medals from the RNLI during his service from 1870 to 1891, in addition to the one he received for the incredibly demanding rescue from the wreck on the Long Sand.

The saving of the crew of the *Indian Chief* by the lifeboat *Bradford* (II) as portrayed by *The Graphic* magazine. In order to save the remaining crew of the Liverpool sailing ship, the tug and lifeboat had to remain at sea for more than twenty-four hours in a winter gale. By daylight, when the Indian Chief had been righted, the wind had increased to strong gale force from the north-east and the sea had become tremendous.

THE MEDAL OF THE INSTITUTION.

Obverse.—Bust of Her Majesty Queen Victoria ; beneath, in minute letters, "L. C. Wyon." Double legend, "Royal National Life-boat Institution. Founded in 1824. Incorporated 1860. Victoria, Patroness."

Reverse.—Three sailors in a Life-boat,—one of whom is in the act of rescuing an exhausted mariner from the waves on a fragment of the wreck. "W. Wyon, Mint." Inscription, "Let not the deep swallow me up."

The design of the Gold and Silver Medals of the Royal National Lifeboat Institution presented to the crews of the Ramsgate lifeboat *Bradford* and tug *Vulcan* after the *Indian Chief* rescue.

The crew of the lifeboat *Bradford* is shown here after the rescue. They are, standing, from left to right: Richard Goldsmith, John Goldsmith, Henry Meader, Tom Cooper Snr., Charles Fish (Cox.), Charles Verrion, Robert Penney, David Berry. Seated: Stephen Goldsmith, Tom Friend, Tom Cooper, Jnr., Henry Belsey.

The seven men from the tug *Vulcan* pictured after receiving their medals. The three seated at centre are believed to be, from left to right: William Wharrier (Engineer), Alf Page (Master), Charles Knight (Mate). Also present are William Austen, Edward Revell, George Woodward and Richard Yare.

Secure in the safety of Ramsgate harbour entrance lies the steam tug *Vulcan* that towed the *Bradford* to its destination in the wild waters of the estuary.

The Duke of Edinburgh presented the medals to the Ramsgate lifeboatmen and tug crew. Popular contemporary author W. Clark Russell wrote a dramatic account of the rescue of the crew of the *Indian Chief*, which served to immortalize the action of the Ramsgate men. It appeared first in the *Daily Telegraph* and has been reproduced many times since.

Last of the pulling and sailing lifeboats at Ramsgate was the *Charles and Susannah Stephens*, which came to the port in 1905 and remained until 1926. Large crowds attended the naming ceremony.

William Cooper was lifeboat coxswain at Ramsgate between 1891 and 1923.

Coxswain Howard Knight and his crew aboard the lifeboat around 1935. They are, from left to right: Walter Read, Douglas Kirkaldie, Tom Read, George Cooper, Edward Knight, Walter Cooper, Alfred Moody, Charles Knight. William Cook, the mechanic, is at the rear and Howard Knight at centre front. He later took the lifeboat *Prudential* to Dunkirk and carried many men from the beaches to rescue vessels waiting offshore.

Douglas Kirkaldie was coxswain of the Ramsgate boat during the years 1946 to 1952. He was awarded a bronze medal from the RNLI for rescuing the crew of another 'Liberty' ship, this time the *Western Farmer*, which broke in half after a collision.

Arthur Verrion was coxswain from 1953 to 1963. He and his crew are here dressed in foul weather gear aboard the lifeboat *Michael and Lily Davis*.

Arthur Verrion enjoys a brief break ashore.

The *Michael and Lily Davis* putting to sea on a call.

The crew of Ramsgate lifeboat enjoy a joke on the cross-wall of the harbour in the 1960s. Those assembled are, from left to right: Ron Cannon Jnr., D. Aves, Bert Pettit, A. Bray, Tommy Cooper (Cox.), Ron Cannon Snr., Herbert Goldfinch, J. Jones, D. Pegden and E. Goldfinch. Ron Cannon Jnr. is currently coxswain of the Ramsgate boat.

North Deal lifeboat *Mary Somerville* being taken from her boathouse which is now headquarters of the Deal Angling Club. The Life Boat Inn next door has long ago disappeared.

Three lifeboats guarded the Downs in the late Victorian period. The coxswains often posed for pictures by W.H. Franklin. They are, from left to right: James Laming (Kingsdown), Richard Roberts (North Deal), Jack Mackins (Walmer). Unfortunately, Franklin's important collection of Victorian and Edwardian shipwreck and lifeboat pictures housed in his premises in Victoria Road, Deal, was lost in the flood of February 1953.

A wreck is reported. A lightvessel sends up a rocket to alert those ashore to the plight of the ship.

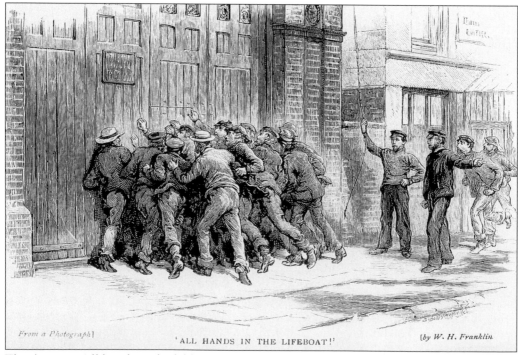

'ALL HANDS IN THE LIFEBOAT!'

The shout is: 'All hands in the lifeboat.' Only those who reached a lifebelt would get a place in it and a portion of any salvage money received.

114

Launch of the *Mary Somerville* as depicted in a contemporary engraving.

Greater reality is captured in this photograph of the *Mary Somerville* entering the water.

The North Deal lifeboat approaches the wreck on the Goodwins.

Amid the turmoil of the sea, flailing cordage and falling spars, a man is saved from the bowsprit of a ship. Victorian engravers created a very realistic impression of the conditions of these rescues.

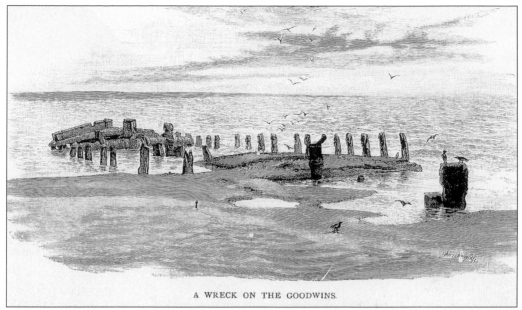

A WRECK ON THE GOODWINS.

All that remained after a few days of bad weather. William Shakespeare in Act III, Scene I of *The Merchant of Venice* described the Sands thus: 'a ship of rich lading wrecked in the Narrow Seas – the Goodwins, I think they call the place; a very dangerous flat and fatal, where the carcasses of many a tall ship lie buried.'

After a successful rescue the crew of the North Deal lifeboat poses for a picture dressed in their cork lifejackets. Those assembled are, from left to right: W. Adams, H. Marsh, W.Gibben, H. Holbourn, T Brown, D. Forster, F. Norris, G. Brown, T. Parsons, P. Paes, R. Budd, F. Roberts, W. Marsh, E. Hanger (second Coxswain), R. Roberts (Coxswain).

A Deal lugger preparing to launch. These extremely seaworthy and robust boats provided many requirements for vessels anchored in the Downs.

There was a prime need for anchors to replace those lost from ships during storms. Launching off the beach in a gale was not easy with six tons of anchor and chain and the *Albion* was wrecked under the pier in the process in December 1867.

In order to provide replacements, lost anchors were recovered after the storm was over.

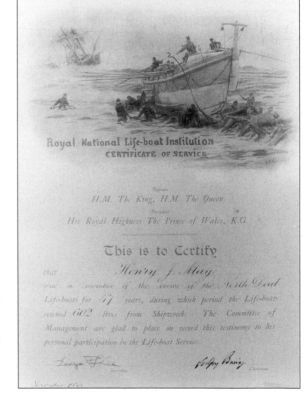

Many men served in the Downs lifeboats from North Deal, Walmer and Kingsdown and most received retirement certificates from the Lifeboat Institution. Henry J. 'Spaniard' May was a member of the crew at North Deal for forty-seven years during which the boats saved 602 lives.

Freddie Upton was coxswain of the Walmer lifeboat during a period of great activity in the post war years. He was awarded two Silver Medals by the RNLI for rescues from large ships wrecked on the Goodwins.

THE LIFEBOAT, WALMER, NEAR DEAL.   61

Freddie Upton's lifeboat the *Charles Dibdin* (*Civil Service No.2*) in the launching position at Walmer. It was stationed there from 1933 to 1959 and rescued 412 lives during that period.

The Walmer crew pictured in front of the lifeboat in 1963. They are, from left to right, standing: -?-, T. Neill, S. Coe (Head Launcher), T. Hurd, F. Morphen, P. Cupperton, Dick Lill, Dan Burton, J. Hurd, Reg. Bailey (second Coxswain), Ben Bailey (Coxswain). Seated: Bruce Brown (Mechanic), R. Rains and C. Hickman.

Last days of the Walmer offshore lifeboat. The *Hampshire Rose* rests on its turntable ready for launching in 1989. The boat was withdrawn the following year when a rigid inflatable inshore lifeboat replaced it.

Alfred Nash

(Inspector of the Dover Police Force),

**Who met his death 11th Sept., 1903, while assisting
to Launch the Lifeboat on a stormy night.**

Good Spirit help us write to-day,
Some soothing, kindly words we pray;
To those who're crushed beneath one blow,
The fatal accident we know.

Inspector Nash's life work's done,
And honours many he has won;
For thirty five years he has been,
On all the beats of Dover seen.

His last great act to try to save,
Some people from a watery grave;
While launching lifeboat did attend,
And Swiftly met his fatal end.

Right nobly on this stormy night,
He tried to do what he thought right;
And there while doing it he found
His own sad death upon the ground.

While always looking well about,
His duty he did carry out;
This night he sought by noble deed,
To help the mariners in need.

By sacrificing his own life,
In aiding others in their strife;
He shows us all the gallant way
In which he ended his life's day.

His Christian walk and manly mien,
By those in Dover long were seen;
Through all these years he won respect,
From every rank and every sect.

To children and to wife so dear,
Be Lord their hope, their stay, their cheer;
In all their anguish and their grief,
Be thou to each their sweet relief.

Console them by thy grace and love,
And grant some day to meet above;
Him whom they loved gone home to hear
The Saviour's welcome word of cheer.

The Police's work is often hard,
And dangers many must they ward
Both day and night with cautious care;
They guard our interest everywhere.

May his long life and noble deed,
Be stimulus in time of need,
To younger men who wish to climb,
The upward ladder in their time.

His comrades all we know so well
Are sorrowful by what's befell;
The Corporation, boatmen, too,
And also Dover folks so true.

We tender all to those he's left,
To wife and children sad bereft,
Our heartfelt prayer for God to bless,
The Widow and the Fatherless.

PRICE ONE PENNY.

Proceeds devoted to the Southern Police Orphanage, Redhill, Surrey

Lives are often saved at a cost. A tribute to a helper killed during a launch of the Dover lifeboat in 1903.

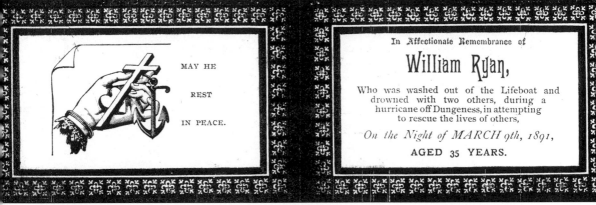

MAY HE

REST

IN PEACE.

In Affectionate Remembrance of

William Ryan,

Who was washed out of the Lifeboat and drowned with two others, during a hurricane off Dungeness, in attempting to rescue the lives of others,

On the Night of MARCH 9th, 1891,

AGED 35 YEARS.

A similar note of remembrance for William Ryan, one of three crewmembers lost from the Dungeness boat in 1891. The Kent coast has a lengthy list of such sacrifices made by boatmen and others in the attempt to save the lives of their fellow men.

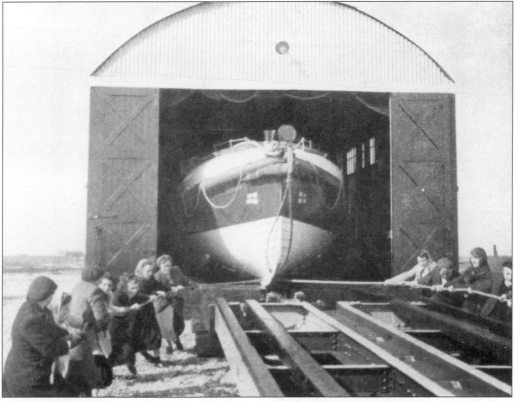

At the southernmost station to serve the Kent coast, the lifeboat has always been launched off the beach as at Walmer, but before the tractor arrived ladies formed a major part of the launching team.

Service boards in Dungeness lifeboat house recall the rescues of one hundred years ago.

In a scene similar to that on the previous page, a group of local ladies swings the more modern lifeboat *Mabel E. Holland* around on its turntable to enable it to be ready to launch again.

The *Mabel E. Holland* assisted the Dutch vessel *Mercurius H*, which went ashore at Dungeness in November 1957.

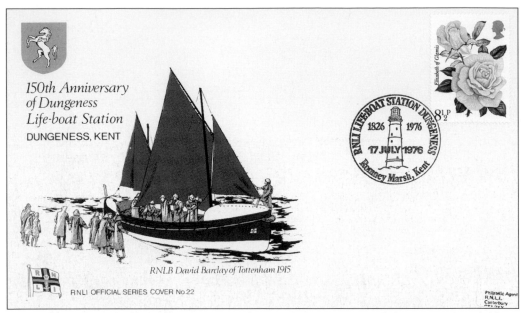

A first day postal cover commemorating the 150th anniversary of the Dungeness lifeboat station. It was issued in 1976. Few details remain from the early days of the station.

The present Dungeness lifeboat house.

Sheerness is the newest station on the Kent coast, having been established in 1970. It is chosen to show examples of modern lifeboats, which have changed a lot from those in use a century ago. The Waveney Class *Helen Turnbull* arrived at Sheerness in 1974.

The *Helen Turnbull* was replaced in September 1996 by the Trent Class boat *George and Ivy Swanson*. Her naming ceremony took place on 11 September 1996.

Acknowledgements

The author would like to express his grateful appreciation to the following photographers whose pictures are reproduced here:

John G. Callis, A. Duncan, Chris Fright, W.H. Franklin, G.E. Houghton, G.W. Jezard, Lambert Weston, Skyfotos (Fotoflite), Mike Jackson, Mike Pett and Tom White.

A number of photographs have been provided by museums and local historians from their collections. The following have been most helpful in this respect: Ramsgate Maritime Museum, Deal Maritime Museum, Dover Museum, Royal National Lifeboat Institution, the World Ship Society, John Reynolds, Mick Twyman, Sid Waldby, John Williams and Terry Williams.

Pictures reproduced from the following publications are also gratefully acknowleged: *The Illustrated London News*, *The Graphic*, *Illustrated Weekly*, *Heroes of the Goodwin Sands* (T.S. Treanor), *The Sea* (F. Whymper), *Isle of Thanet Gazette* and *Folkestone Herald*.

Certain pictures have previously been published in the monthly publications, *Sea Breezes* and *Bygone Kent* in support of longer articles by Anthony Lane about those particular shipwrecks.